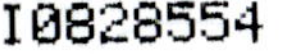

John Vianney

Saint for Holy Orders

(Also known as the Curé of Ars)

1786-1859

Born in Dardilly, France

Feast Day: August 4

Patron saint of parish priests and confessors

Dedication

To my family:
my parents Jim and Peg,
my husband Bill,
our son Sam and daughter-in-law Erin,
and our precious grandchildren
Ben, Lucas, and Andrew

To all the children I have had the privilege
of teaching throughout the years.

And to priests who shepherd the People of God
and bring us closer to Christ.

Imprimi Potest:
Stephen T. Rehrauer, CSsR, Provincial
Denver Province, The Redemptorists

Imprimatur:
In accordance with CIC 827, permission to publish has been granted on February 5, 2018, by the Most Reverend Mark S. Rivituso, Auxiliary Bishop, Archdiocese of St. Louis. Permission to publish is an indication that nothing contrary to Church teaching is contained in this work. It does not imply any endorsement of the opinions expressed in the publication; nor is any liability assumed by this permission.

Published by Liguori Publications, Liguori, Missouri 63057

To order, visit Liguori.org or call 800-325-9521.

ISBN 978-0-7648-2795-2

Liguori Publications, a nonprofit corporation, is an apostolate of the Redemptorists. To learn more about the Redemptorists, visit Redemptorists.com.

Printed in the United States of America
22 21 20 19 18 / 5 4 3 2 1
First Edition

Dear Parents and Teachers:

Saints and Me! is a series of children's books about saints, with six books apiece in the first four sets. The first set, *Saints of North America,* honors holy men and women who blessed and served the land we call home. The second, *Saints of Christmas*, includes heavenly heroes who inspire us through Advent and Christmas and teach us to love the Infant Jesus. The third, *Saints for Families*, introduces saints who modeled God's love within and for the domestic Church. The fourth, *Saints for Communities,* explores individuals from different times and places who served Jesus through their various roles and professions.

The seven books in the *Saints for Sacraments* series explore eight saints who had great love for the sacraments. John the Baptist baptized Jesus in the Jordan River. Padre Pio helped people make a good confession. Teresa of Ávila was known for her great love of the Eucharist. Philip Neri received the Holy Spirit after praying to God. Louis and Zélie Martin, a married couple, taught their children to serve God and the poor. At an early age, John Vianney wanted to dedicate his life to God as a priest; today he is the patron saint of parish priests. Maximilian Kolbe battled poor health to become a priest and brought God's healing to sick people.

Name the saint who lived in the desert and ate locusts and honey. In this set of books, who was the saint with stigmata? Who began a Carmelite convent dedicated to prayer? Who grew up during the French Revolution? Which saints were the parents of Thérèse of Lisieux? Who volunteered to die in place of a stranger in a prison camp? Find out in the *Saints for Sacraments* set—part of the *Saints and Me!* series—and help children connect to the lives of the saints.

Introduce your children or students to the *Saints and Me!* series as they:

—**READ** about the lives of the saints and are inspired by their stories.

—**PRAY** to the saints for their intercession.

—**CELEBRATE** the saints and relate them to their lives.

Saints for Sacraments

John the Baptist
Baptism

Teresa of Ávila
Eucharist

Philip Neri
Confirmation

Padre Pio
Reconciliation

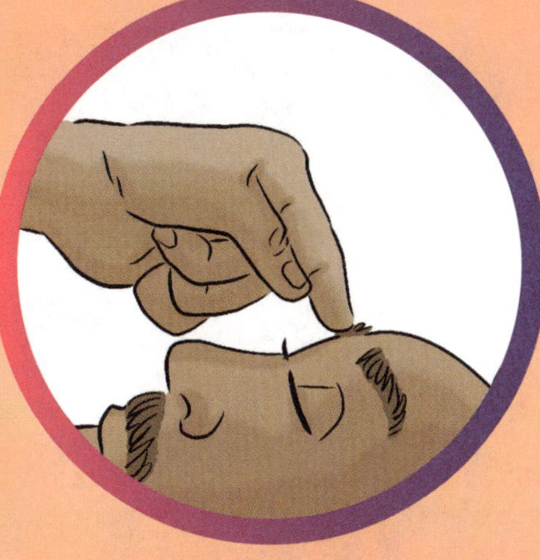

Maximilian Kolbe
Anointing of the Sick

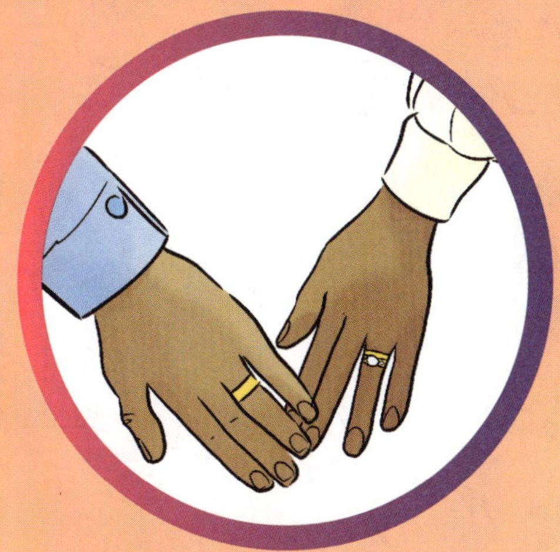

Louis and Zélie Martin
Matrimony

John Vianney
Holy Orders

A vocation is a special calling from God to live a holy life. John Vianney chose to live a holy life as a parish priest and pastor. He received holy orders, a sacrament of service to others. John Vianney grew in holiness as he faithfully served the people of God.

John was born in 1786 in the small town of Dardilly, France. He was a shepherd on his family's farm. He took care of the sheep, leading them to the fields and the hillside. While the sheep grazed, John liked to pray. Praying helped him feel close to Jesus.

When John was young, a terrible war was taking place in France. The war brought many changes. Churches were closed. People practiced their faith in secret. Priests had to hide or they were put in jail! John made his first Communion in secret when he was thirteen years old.

Thankfully, the war ended and churches opened again. John, now in his late teens, felt God calling him to be a priest. A priest says Mass, baptizes, and hears confessions. He gives advice and helps people grow in their faith. "I want to be a priest so I can help people love God," John told his parents.

POOR!

John entered the seminary. There were many important lessons for the shepherd boy to learn. John studied every day, but the work was hard to understand. The tests were hard, too! John prayed, "God, please help me." He kept trying and did not give up!

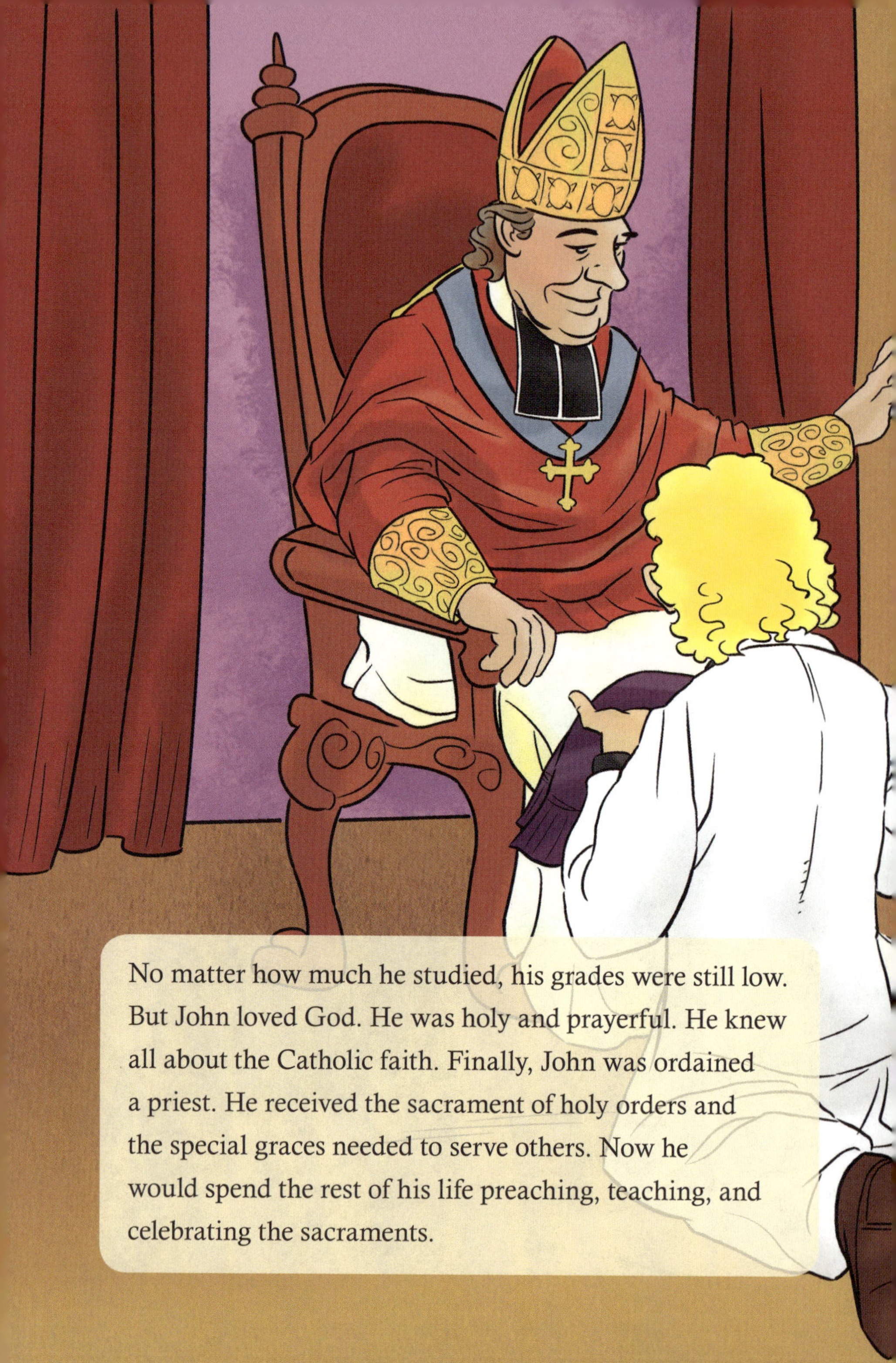

No matter how much he studied, his grades were still low. But John loved God. He was holy and prayerful. He knew all about the Catholic faith. Finally, John was ordained a priest. He received the sacrament of holy orders and the special graces needed to serve others. Now he would spend the rest of his life preaching, teaching, and celebrating the sacraments.

Father Vianney first served in a village near Dardilly. Later he was sent to Ars, a small farming village. Only a few hundred people lived there. The bishop told Father Vianney, "The people in the village of Ars do not love God. You will have to help them." "I promise you, I will help them. I will lead the people to Jesus," he said.

He set off for the village of Ars. Seeing a young boy on the road, he asked, "Is this the way to Ars?" The boy smiled, pointed his finger, and said, "That way, Father." He walked a short distance, knelt down and prayed, "God, help me to be a good and holy priest!"

Father Vianney had a lot of work to do! Some people worked on Sunday instead of going to Mass. They liked to go to dances and parties. He heard some of them say bad words. Over the years, the people of Ars had lost their Catholic faith. Father Vianney would help them find it.

He visited people in their homes and talked to them about their life on the farm. They shared their problems with him and he always took time to listen. He visited the sick and prayed with them. Through his words and actions, Father Vianney taught people how to live and love like Jesus.

"Come to Mass, and come meet Jesus," he urged. His homilies were simple and easy to understand. People received holy Communion. Many people wanted to go to confession. Father Vianney heard confessions for several hours every day. He knew what was in the people's hearts and he helped them feel the joy of God's forgiveness. Slowly, the people of Ars came back to the Church.

Lots of stories were told about the kind and humble priest. Soon people from many places came to see Father Vianney. Now he heard more confessions, spending up to sixteen hours in his confessional each day.

A railroad line was built so people could go to Ars to visit with Father Vianney, talk to him, or go to confession. They waited many hours, sometimes days. But they did not mind. Father Vianney, a loving and faithful priest, helped them grow close to God.

John Vianney was once a shepherd on his family's farm. When he grew up, he became the Good Shepherd of God's people. Father John Vianney kept his promise to lead people to Jesus. After forty-one years as pastor of Ars, he died peacefully in his room with friends at his bedside. He was canonized by Pope Pius XI in 1925, and later named the patron saint of parish priests.

"The priesthood is the love of the heart of Jesus. When you see a priest, think of our Lord Jesus Christ."

—Father John Vianney

Saint John Vianney,
you loved God with
all your heart.
You brought many people to
him by your words
and actions.
Help me to be humble
and holy like you,
so I can help other people.
Amen.

Everything you do, everything you say,
Do it for the love of God today.

GLOSSARY (NEW WORDS)

Ars: A small village in southeast France, also known as Ars-sur-Formans

Bishop: A priest who is the leader of many churches in a certain area

Confessional: A booth, small room, or area where a priest hears confessions

Curé: The French word for "parish priest"

Dardilly: A town in France near Ars

Holy Orders: A sacrament of service. A baptized man is ordained to serve the Church as a deacon, priest, or bishop

Homily: A short talk about the meaning of the readings heard at Mass

Ordination: To receive the sacrament of holy orders and become a deacon, priest, or bishop

Parish: A faith community led by a pastor

Pastor: A priest who leads a parish

Priest: An ordained minister who celebrates the sacraments, preaches the gospel, and takes care of God's people

Sacraments: The seven special signs of God's life and love

Seminary: A school where men are trained to be priests

Vocation: A call from God to serve him in a special way